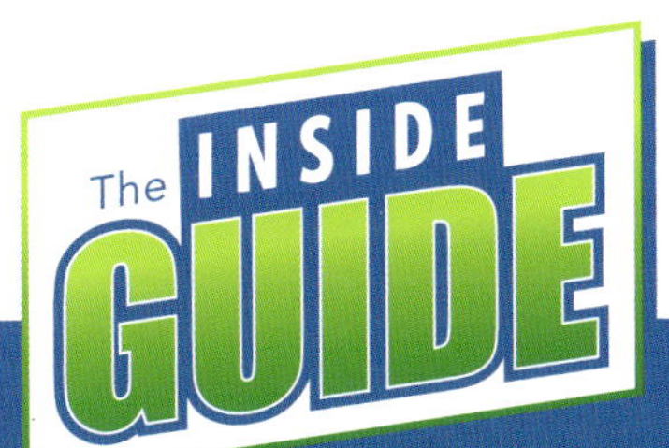

CIVIL RIGHTS HEROES

Jesse Jackson

By Amy B. Rogers

New York

Published in 2022 by Cavendish Square Publishing, LLC
29 E. 21st Street, New York, NY 10010

First Edition

Portions of this work were originally authored by Barbara M. Linde and published as *Jesse Jackson* (*Civil Rights Crusaders*).
All new material this edition authored by Amy B. Rogers.

Library of Congress Cataloging-in-Publication Data
Names: Rogers, Amy B., author.
Title: Jesse Jackson / Amy B. Rogers.
Description: New York : Cavendish Square Publishing, [2022] | Series: The inside guide: civil rights heroes | Includes bibliographical references and index.
Identifiers: LCCN 2020030083 | ISBN 9781502660244 (library binding) | ISBN 9781502660220 (paperback) | ISBN 9781502660237 (set) | ISBN 9781502660251 (ebook)
Subjects: LCSH: Jackson, Jesse, 1941—Juvenile literature. | African American civil rights workers–Biography–Juvenile literature. | African American presidential candidates–Biography–Juvenile literature. | Civil rights–United States–History–Juvenile literature.
Classification: LCC E185.97.J25 R64 2022 | DDC 323.092 [B]–dc23
LC record available at https://lccn.loc.gov/2020030083

Editor: Katie Kawa
Copy Editor: Abby Young
Designer: Andrea Davison-Bartolotta

The photographs in this book are used by permission and through the courtesy of: Cover, p. 12 Bettmann/Getty Images; p. 4 Brett Carlsen/Getty Images; p. 6 Joe Klamar/AFP via Getty Images; p. 7 Don Carl Steffen/Gamma-Rapho via Getty Images; p. 8 Scott Heins/Getty Images; p. 9 Bill Pugliano/Getty Images; pp. 10, 29 (bottom) Jacques M. Chenet/CORBIS/Corbis via Getty Images; p. 13 Courtesy of the Library of Congress; p. 14 Michael Mauney/The LIFE Images Collection via Getty Images/ Getty Images; p. 15 Joe Raedle/Getty Images; p. 16 Robert Abbott Sengstacke/Getty Images; p. 18 Diana Walker/The LIFE Images Collection via Getty Images; p. 19 Michael Tighe/Donaldson Collection/Getty Images; p. 20 Peter Turnley/Corbis/ VCG via Getty Images; p. 21 Jon Levy/AFP via Getty Images; p. 22 Jeff Haynes/AFP via Getty Images; p. 23 Stan Honda/AFP via Getty Images; p. 24 Stephen Maturen/Getty Images; p. 25 Johnny Nunez/WireImage/Getty Images; p. 26 Tim Boyle/Getty Images; p. 27 Paul J. Richards/AFP via Getty Images; p. 28 (top left) Wally McNamee/CORBIS/Corbis via Getty Images; p. 28 (bottom left) Steve Liss/The LIFE Images Collection via Getty Images/Getty Images; p. 28 (top right) White House/AFP via Getty Images; p. 28 (bottom right) sinology/Moment/Getty Images; p. 29 (top) Stephen F. Somerstein/Getty Images.

Some of the images in this book illustrate individuals who are models. The depictions do not imply actual situations or events.

CPSIA compliance information: Batch #CS22CSQ: For further information contact Cavendish Square Publishing LLC, New York, New York, at 1-877-980-4450.

Printed in the United States of America

CONTENTS

Jesse Jackson was active in the civil rights movement of the 1950s and 1960s, and he has continued to stand up for the rights of Black Americans into the 21st century. He's shown here at a protest against police violence in 2020.

CONTINUING THE FIGHT

The civil rights movement changed the United States forever. It called attention to the unfair and unequal treatment of Black Americans and led to important changes, such as the end of legal segregation. However, it reached its peak more than 50 years ago, and many of the men and women who led the movement are no longer alive. It's hard to know how they would react to the problems Black Americans are still facing today.

This is why it's important to listen to the civil rights leaders who are still speaking out, such as Jesse Jackson. He's carrying on the **legacy** of his fellow civil rights heroes who changed the country in the 1950s and 1960s.

Fast Fact

Segregation was the forced separation of Black Americans and white Americans through laws known as Jim Crow laws. Black Americans had to use separate restaurants, hotels, schools, and other facilities in many parts of the United States, especially the South.

Jesse and Martin

One of the most famous leaders of the civil rights movement was Dr. Martin Luther King Jr. He inspired many young people to become more active in the fight for civil rights. Jesse was one of those young people.

Martin was a **mentor** to Jesse, and Jesse worked with him until Martin's death in 1968. Jesse's continued activism is an important link between the past and the future of the fight for justice and equality for Black Americans. Just as Martin inspired him, he has inspired new generations of young activists.

A Strong Voice

Martin was one civil rights leader who was killed in the 1960s. Malcolm X—a more **militant** voice for Black pride and power—was another. Although these men could never be replaced, Jesse has followed in their footsteps as a powerful speaker and activist.

Jesse has become a leading voice on issues affecting Black Americans. He continues to call attention to examples of racism and injustice, reminding all Americans that the fight for equality didn't end in the 1960s.

Jesse has continued to help keep Martin's legacy alive. He can be seen here at the Martin Luther King, Jr. Memorial in Washington, D.C., honoring his mentor.

Fast Fact

Jesse shares his thoughts in speeches and interviews, and he shares them on social media too. He joined Twitter in 2009, and he also has his own Facebook page.

Jesse has carried on the tradition of giving powerful speeches to inspire others to become more active in the fight for civil rights and against racism.

Equality for All

In a speech in 1988, Jesse said, "America is not a blanket woven from one thread, one color, one cloth." He believes that it takes all kinds of people to make America a strong, successful, and great country.

Jesse has often spoken out about the importance of accepting all people and working to protect the rights of all Americans, especially those who've been treated unfairly. This includes Black Americans, women, members of the **LGBTQ+ community**, and many others.

THE REALITY OF RACISM

Jesse has spoken out against racism for much of his life. Racism is the belief that one race is better than others and should get better treatment because of this. It also describes governments and social systems that are founded on this belief and allow it to continue.

In the United States, racism is a systemic problem. This means that it affects almost every aspect of life—from education and housing to jobs and health care. White Americans are the race that has been in power from the founding of the country, so people of other races often deal with discrimination—unfair and unequal treatment—because of their race.

The Black Lives Matter movement was started to call attention to the continued problem of systemic racism in the United States, especially the issue of police violence against Black Americans.

Still Speaking Out

Jesse continues to serve as an important voice in the fight against racism. His words carry weight because they're spoken by a man who's lived through segregation, the deaths of many of his fellow civil rights leaders, and the continued struggle for Black Americans to achieve equality.

Jesse has spent his life fighting for what he believes is right. That fight has taken him from the segregated South to powerful positions that have allowed him to help others around the world.

Fast Fact

Jesse has spoken at the funerals of famous Black Americans, including singer Aretha Franklin, as well as the funerals of Black Americans who've died because of police violence.

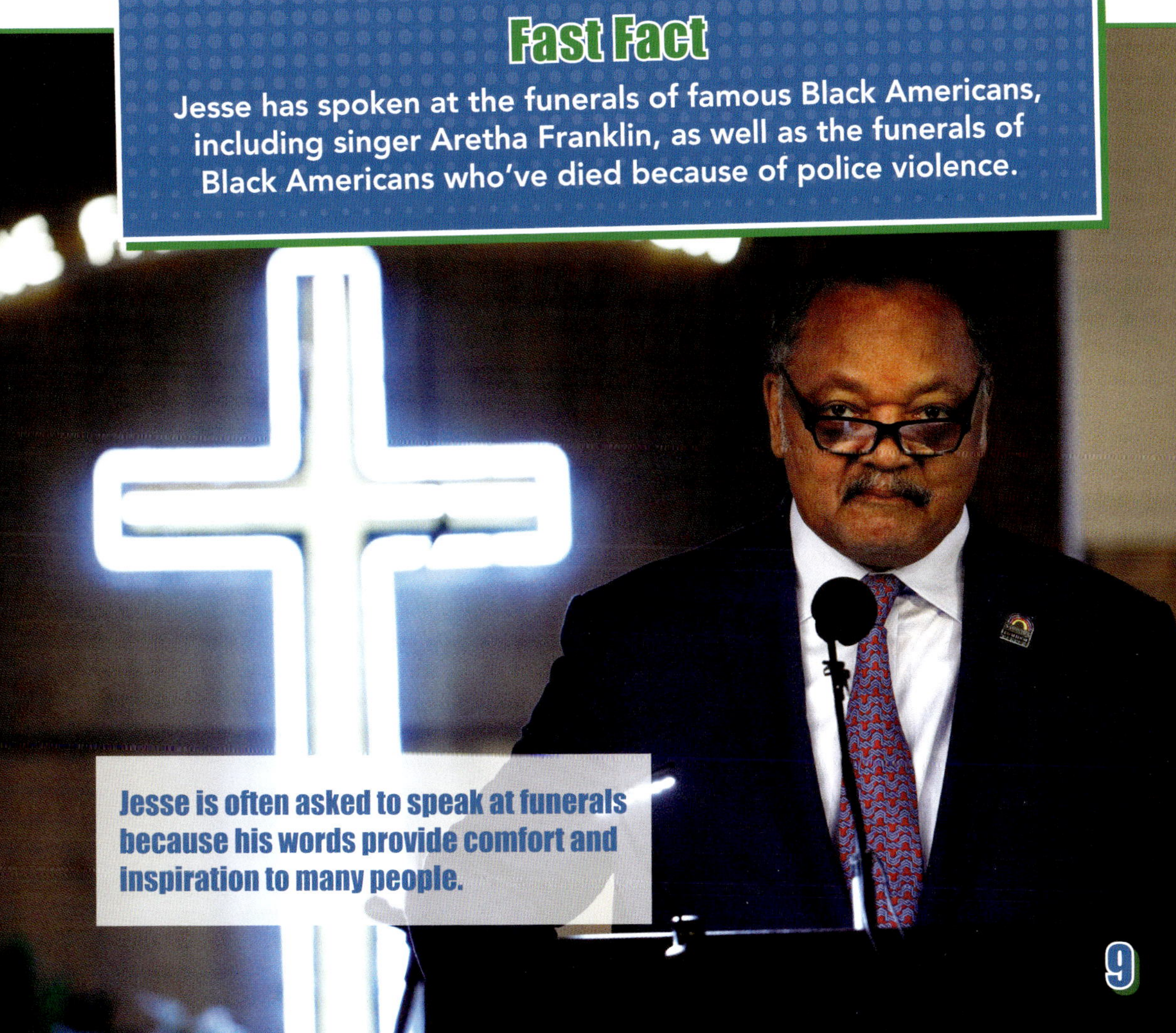

Jesse is often asked to speak at funerals because his words provide comfort and inspiration to many people.

Jesse's childhood helped shape him into the activist he became. He understands the importance of helping young people succeed.

A YOUNG ACTIVIST

Jesse Louis Burns was born on October 8, 1941. He eventually took the last name of his stepfather, Charles Jackson. Jesse grew up in Greenville, South Carolina, and he was surrounded by the effects of segregation, especially at school. Although his school wasn't as nice as the schools for white children in Greenville, Jesse still worked hard. The classroom was where his path to success began.

School Days

Jesse did well in school. He played sports and got good grades. He was even elected class president!

Jesse started college at the University of Illinois, which was made up of mostly white students. After a year, he switched schools and started at the Agricultural and Technical College of North Carolina, which had mostly Black students. During Jesse's time in college, he became active in the civil rights movement in North Carolina. By the time he graduated in 1964, he was ready to help in bigger ways.

Fast Fact

After Jesse finished college in North Carolina, he studied to become a minister in Chicago, Illinois. In 1968, he officially became a Baptist minister, which is why he's sometimes known as the Reverend Jesse Jackson.

STARTING A SIT-IN

When Jesse was home on a break from college, he needed to borrow books for a school project. He visited the library in Greenville that Black people could use, but it didn't have enough books on the subject. However, when he tried to go to the library for white people, he was told he couldn't get any books by himself, and police officers were there waiting for him.

Jesse knew this was unfair, and he wanted to do something about it. In July 1960, he and seven other students staged a sit-in at the library for white people. They started reading and didn't leave until they were arrested.

Sit-ins were a popular form of protest during the civil rights movement. Black people sat in places that were supposed to be for white people only and refused to move. This was a form of civil disobedience—peacefully refusing to follow a law that is unfair or unjust.

Starting in Selma

In 1965, Martin Luther King Jr. and other civil rights leaders planned a march from Selma to Montgomery in Alabama to call attention to the problems Black Americans had registering to vote. Jesse joined them in Selma and soon started working as part of the Southern Christian Leadership Conference (SCLC).

Martin led the SCLC in its work fighting for civil rights. He took a chance on Jesse and gave him a job helping the SCLC in Chicago. Jesse became a full-time member of the civil rights movement.

Fast Fact

Jesse married Jacqueline Lavinia Brown in 1962. They raised five children together.

Jesse spent many years working with the SCLC and met many other civil rights leaders during his time with this organization.

Operation Breadbasket

In Chicago, Jesse helped set up the city's branch of Operation Breadbasket. This part of the SCLC focused on providing economic help to Black Americans. It did this by supporting Black-owned businesses. It also helped organize **boycotts** of white businesses that refused to hire Black workers.

Jesse was so successful with Operation Breadbasket in Chicago that he was put in charge of the whole program. When Martin talked about Jesse's success, he said, "We knew he was going to do a good job, but he's done better than a good job."

Jesse is shown here speaking at an event for Operation Breadbasket.

The Loss of a Mentor

Martin was one of Jesse's mentors, and Martin was often impressed with Jesse's work. However, they didn't always agree. Martin sometimes felt Jesse was focused too much on his own vision for America's future and not on what was best for everyone.

Even though they sometimes argued, Martin and Jesse still worked together. In fact, they were both in Memphis, Tennessee, on April 4, 1968. This was the day Martin was shot and killed at the Lorraine Motel. Jesse claimed he was the last person to talk to Martin. Not everyone believed his story, but it was clear that Martin had played an important part in Jesse's life.

Fast Fact

Today, the National Civil Rights Museum is located at the site of what was once the Lorraine Motel.

Jesse returned to the location of the Lorraine Motel in Memphis in 2018 to honor Martin's life 50 years after his death.

Jesse is shown here reading a newspaper from the day after Martin's death. After that tragic day, Jesse continued to work for justice and equality. Martin was gone, but Jesse kept fighting.

PUSHING FOR EQUALITY

The murder of Martin Luther King Jr. was a national tragedy. It was also a deeply personal loss for Jesse. He had lost his friend and mentor, but he didn't let that stop him from continuing Martin's work. In fact, in the years after Martin's death, Jesse was busier than ever before as he started new projects, traveled the world, and even ran for president.

A New Group

Jesse continued to run Operation Breadbasket after Martin's death. However, he didn't always get along well with other members of the SCLC. In 1971, he officially left the group and founded a new organization called Operation PUSH (People United to Save Humanity).

Operation PUSH was created to help Black Americans help themselves by providing economic and educational help to those who need it. One important part of PUSH is known as Push for Excellence, Inc. (often shortened to PUSH Excel). The goal of PUSH Excel is to help students succeed in school and learn to believe in themselves.

Fast Fact
PUSH Excel started in 1975 and is still helping students today.

Running for President

In 1984, Jesse started the National Rainbow Coalition. Jesse explained the name of this organization by saying, "Our flag is red, white, and blue, but our nation is a rainbow—red, yellow, brown, black, and white." The National Rainbow Coalition represented many groups, including women, Black Americans, and members of the LGBTQ+ community.

Jesse wanted to change the country in big ways, so he decided to run for president. In 1984 and 1988, he campaigned to be the Democratic Party's candidate for president. He didn't win the party's **nomination** in either year. However, he did make Democratic leaders more aware of issues affecting Black voters.

Fast Fact

In 1996, the Rainbow Coalition and Operation PUSH merged, or joined, to become one organization. It's now known as the Rainbow PUSH (or Rainbow/PUSH) Coalition.

Jesse's presidential campaigns showed that many Americans would support a Black president. However, it took 20 more years before Barack Obama made Jesse's dream a reality.

SHIRLEY CHISHOLM

Jesse Jackson was the first Black man to run for president as part of one of the two main **political parties** in the United States (the Democratic Party and the Republican Party). However, a Black woman did this before him! In 1972, Shirley Chisholm campaigned to be the Democratic Party's candidate for U.S. president. Like Jesse, she didn't become the party's **nominee**, but she paved the way for the men and women who came after her.

Shirley was also the first Black woman to be elected to Congress in the United States. She died in 2005, but her legacy of groundbreaking leadership lives on today.

Shirley Chisholm's story is an important part of American history.

Traveling the World

Jesse's presidential campaigns and **social justice** work put him in the national spotlight, and world leaders took notice. Jesse was sometimes sent to other countries to help solve international problems. He also helped raise awareness about important issues around the world. For example, in 1997, President Bill Clinton sent him to Africa, where he talked to leaders about freedom and equality for all people.

Fast Fact

Jesse traveled to South Africa in 1979 to speak out against the policy of apartheid in that country. Apartheid allowed for legal segregation of the races and discrimination against South Africans who weren't white.

Jesse is shown here visiting children in Africa. Helping people around the world is very important to him.

Jesse sometimes helped bring back Americans who were prisoners in other countries, including Syria and Iraq. He has also traveled to many different places to give speeches about social justice.

The Wall Street Project

Even though Jesse traveled around the world and campaigned for the country's highest political office, he didn't forget his roots. One of his first contributions to the civil rights movement was his leadership of Operation Breadbasket. In 1996, Jesse returned to the idea of providing economic help to Black Americans when he started the Wall Street Project.

The Wall Street Project is part of the Rainbow PUSH Coalition. It supports businesses owned by Black Americans, and it works toward economic equality for all Americans.

Jesse's work through the Wall Street Project also supports businesses run by women.

Jesse is shown here with President Barack Obama. Both men worked to help the Black community in Chicago before turning their attention to the nation as a whole.

PAST, PRESENT, AND FUTURE

In 2008, Jesse was shown crying tears of joy when Barack Obama was elected president of the United States—the country's first Black president. Jesse's presidential campaigns had helped pave the way for Barack's success, and he supported and campaigned for Barack too.

Jesse's work isn't just a part of history. He's still actively working to make the United States a place where everyone is treated fairly.

Jesse is shown here after it was announced that Barack Obama had won the 2008 presidential election.

Fast Fact

Jesse also has a connection to Michelle Obama, who was the First Lady during Barack's time as president. Michelle became friends with Jesse's daughter Santita when they were younger.

A Difficult Disease

In 2017, Jesse announced that he has Parkinson's disease. This is a disease that affects the **nervous system** and causes problems with movement, including shaking and stiffness. Although Parkinson's disease is a serious illness, Jesse hasn't let it stop him from spreading his message of hope, equality, and justice across the country.

In fact, Jesse has stated that he believes his illness can help him help others by raising awareness about Parkinson's disease. He said, "It is an opportunity for me to use my voice to help in finding a cure." Helping others continues to be Jesse's focus.

Writing and Speaking

Jesse hasn't let his illness keep him from working. He still travels to speak at funerals, protests, and other events. For example, in 2020, Jesse traveled to Minneapolis, Minnesota, which was where a Black man named George Floyd was killed by police officers. George's death led to many protests in that city and across the country. Jesse encouraged the protesters, saying, "The protests must continue, but around the country ... protest until something happens."

Jesse attended a memorial service for George Floyd in Minneapolis in June 2020.

AL SHARPTON

Jesse is one of the most famous Black Americans fighting for justice today. Another leader in this fight is Al Sharpton. The two men have known each other for many years. In fact, Jesse gave Al a job in 1969 as the youth director for Operation Breadbasket. Jesse is often seen as a mentor to Al in the way Martin Luther King Jr. was to Jesse.

Today, Al is the leader of the National Action Network (NAN), which is a civil rights organization. He also hosts radio shows and a television program, and he has interviewed Jesse about modern civil rights issues.

Jesse and Al have often worked together to raise awareness about issues affecting Black Americans.

Jesse has also shared his thoughts and feelings by writing about them. He has written for newspapers, and he has also written books.

Fast Fact

In 2019, Jesse worked with Grace Kim to create a book of speeches he has given throughout his life. It's titled *Keeping Hope Alive: Sermons and Speeches of Rev. Jesse L. Jackson, Sr.*

The Coalition Continues

The Rainbow PUSH Coalition is an important part of Jesse's legacy of service and leadership. It's still an active part of the communities it serves today.

For example, during the **COVID-19 pandemic**, which reached the United States in 2020, the Rainbow PUSH Coalition provided information about sites where people could get tested for the disease. It also helped provide food and financial resources for many people who'd lost their jobs during the pandemic. Jesse's sense of community service, which began on a national level with Operation Breadbasket, continues to influence the work done by this organization.

Jesse is still helping young people through the Rainbow PUSH Coalition and especially its PUSH Excel program.

"Go Forward"

In 1988, Jesse gave a speech in which he said, "Never surrender, young America. Go forward." Jesse has followed that advice for his entire life. As a young man, he could have surrendered when faced with segregation and discrimination. However, he continued to go forward. He kept going forward after the death of his mentor and after his presidential campaigns failed. He continues to go forward today, even after being diagnosed with a serious illness.

Jesse has never given up when he's faced hard times. He inspires people to keep going forward on the path toward justice and equality.

Fast Fact

In 2000, President Bill Clinton awarded Jesse the Presidential Medal of Freedom. This is the highest award a president can give to a civilian.

Jesse once said to young Americans, "You must never stop dreaming." He believes in the power of the next generation to change the world for the better.

TIMELINE

In Jesse's Life

1941
Jesse is born on October 8 in Greenville, South Carolina.

1965
Jesse joins the SCLC.

1971
Jesse founds Operation PUSH.

1984
Jesse founds the National Rainbow Coalition and runs for U.S. president.

1988
Jesse runs for president a second time.

2020
Jesse speaks to protesters in Minneapolis after the death of George Floyd.

In the World

1939–1945
World War II is fought.

1968
Martin Luther King Jr. is killed.

1974
Richard Nixon resigns, or steps down, from his job as U.S. president.

2008
Barack Obama becomes the first African American to be elected U.S. president.

2019–2020
The COVID-19 pandemic begins in China and spreads around the world.

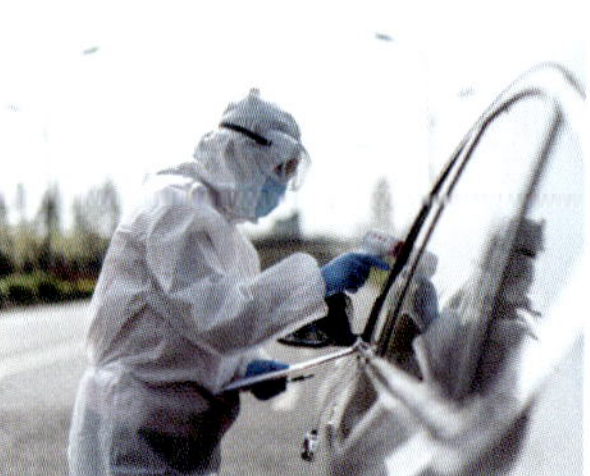

THINK ABOUT IT!

1. Martin Luther King Jr. was an important mentor in Jesse's life. Who do you look up to? How can you use what they've taught you to make the world a better place?

2. What do you think inspired Jesse to travel to Selma to begin working with the SCLC?

3. How did Jesse Jackson and Shirley Chisholm pave the way for future Black leaders such as Barack Obama?

4. What part of Jesse's story inspired you the most?

GLOSSARY

boycott: The act of joining with others in refusing to deal with someone or support a business as a form of protest.

civilian: A person not on active duty in the military.

COVID-19 pandemic: An event that began in China in 2019 in which a disease that causes breathing problems, a fever, and other health issues spread rapidly around the world and made millions of people sick in a short period of time.

legacy: The lasting effect of a person or thing.

LGBTQ+ community: A group made up of people who see themselves as a gender different from the sex they were assigned at birth or who want to be in romantic relationships that aren't only male-female. LGBTQ stands for lesbian, gay, bisexual, transgender, and queer or questioning.

mentor: A person who teaches, gives guidance, or gives advice to someone, especially a less experienced person.

militant: Using force to support a cause or beliefs.

nervous system: The part of the body that deals with sending messages for controlling feeling and movement between the brain and the rest of the body using nerves.

nomination: The act of choosing a candidate for an election.

nominee: A person who has been formally chosen as a candidate for a political office.

political party: A group whose members hold the same general beliefs about how government should work.

social justice: The concept of fair and equal treatment of people in a society.

FIND OUT MORE

Books

Braun, Eric. *The Civil Rights Movement*. Minneapolis, MN: Lerner Publications, 2019.

O'Mara, John. *The Civil Rights Movement*. New York, NY: Gareth Stevens Publishing, 2020.

The Staff of The Undefeated. *The Fierce 44: Black Americans Who Shook Up the World*. Boston, MA: HMH Books for Young Readers, 2019.

Websites

International Civil Rights Walk of Fame
www.nps.gov/features/malu/feat0002/wof/index.htm
Visitors to this website can read short biographies about many different civil rights heroes, including Martin Luther King Jr. and Jesse Jackson.

Jesse Jackson: Chronology
www.pbs.org/wgbh/pages/frontline/jesse/chronology.html
This part of the PBS website features a timeline of events in Jesse's life, focusing on his activism in the 20th century.

PUSH Excel
www.pushexcel.org/
The official PUSH Excel website offers information about how this organization continues to help young people today.

Publisher's note to educators and parents: Our editors have carefully reviewed these websites to ensure that they are suitable for students. Many websites change frequently, however, and we cannot guarantee that a site's future contents will continue to meet our high standards of quality and educational value. Be advised that students should be closely supervised whenever they access the Internet.

INDEX